CON TEM PLA TIVE MAN

BROCK GUTHRIE

SIBLING RIVALRY PRESS
ALEXANDER, ARKANSAS
WWW.SIBLINGRIVALRYPRESS.COM

Contemplative Man

Copyright © 2014 by Brock Guthrie

Author photo: Brooke Champagne. Used by permission.

Cover design: Seth Pennington

All rights reserved. No part of this book may be reproduced or republished without written consent from the publisher, except by reviewers who may quote brief excerpts in connection with a review in a newspaper, magazine, or electronic publication; nor may any part of this book be reproduced, stored in a retrieval system, or transmitted in any form, or by any means be recorded without written consent of the publisher.

Sibling Rivalry Press, LLC
13913 Magnolia Glen Drive
Alexander, AR 72002

info@siblingrivalrypress.com

www.siblingrivalrypress.com

ISBN: 978-1-937420-67-3

Library of Congress Control Number: 2013956733

First Sibling Rivalry Press Edition, March 2014

For **BROOKE**

CONTENTS

BUT WHAT IS THERE TO SAY?

12 Some Days
14 Circle K Blues
15 Thing Is, I Love Spicy Food
16 Really Good Salsa
18 I'm the Asshole
20 Catch and Release
24 Trial Membership
26 Pose Poem
28 A Good Moment
30 Ode to Stanley
31 Lukewarm Coffee
34 The Long Run
36 Small Bar

SAINT RANDY OF THE SODDEN BAR NAPKIN

- **40** All That Water
- **41** Shiver
- **43** Fishing with Paul
- **45** Watch Those PMs
- **46** Anna Nicole Has Collapsed
- **47** Something to Look At
- **49** Roofer
- **52** Appropriate Interjection
- **54** He Quits His Blue-Collar Job
- **55** Candy Dish
- **58** Loving Cup
- **59** Religion
- **61** The Wagon

ERRANDS

- **64** Once I Get Up This Hill
- **65** Clever Fish
- **66** Poetry
- **67** Airplane Asshole
- **69** Antizigzag
- **70** Errands
- **72** Shh . . . We're Trying to Focus in Here
- **73** July Fourth
- **76** Animals
- **80** Brush Clearing
- **83** Half Hour

CONTEMPLATIVE MAN

BUT WHAT IS THERE TO SAY?

SOME DAYS

Some days more than others I'm willing to put my
two-cents in—say what I'm thinking if I'm thinking without
hesitation. Like when I'm paying for groceries or paying
for something else. Looking for an answer. Anywhere
people wait in line and I'm one of those people
and there's a person in charge. Maybe I'm talking
about the clerk, totally jovial, whose employee manual
possibly includes "chat with the customer"
or something hopeful like that. When I'm in those lines
I'm often convinced these guys really mean it—
and the customers, too. Good for them. Because some days
I could mean it. But others I don't and therefore
stay silent, even if, for instance, there's a girl in front of me
at the hardware store buying furnace filters, wood glue,
    a keychain flashlight
she noticed, as I did, in that jar near the cash register,
and she's pretty in a smart way, you know, a subtle way
that's maddening, and she asks a non-hardware question
like directions to a restaurant, or if it's any good.
And the clerk's desperate to help, but he's foreign
and lacks a native's answer. But I, in my aloofness,
could be sitting on a good one, a two-to-eight-word answer
that says it all about that restaurant, an answer she'd
appreciate for its concision, the same one I wouldn't give
that could persuade her to remember me later. Am I
the kind of contemplative man I never cared for as a boy?
I was a contemplative boy, but didn't know it then. But now
I meet a clerk at the gas station who rings up my wine,
    my cigarettes,

my scratch-offs, and he's got a friend behind the counter
who clearly doesn't work here. A girl. Appealing.
Looks natural and appealing doing what she's doing, which is
reading the clerk's poem, one that he wrote, in front of him
while he says things interruptive like: *I tried something there,
but I don't know if it works.* And I'm having
the kind of day . . . I'm feeling words are inadequate,
but here's a guy with a friend who reads his poems
    in a gas station!
Something false inside me wants to spill out,
and I feel the need to express something definitive,
but instead it's: *So you like that shit, do you?*
And the girl continues reading as though my comment
    couldn't matter
but the clerk's a tactful bastard. Tells me it's OK. Tells me
I'd have to write them to "truly understand." Tells me
he has *intelligent friends who just don't get poetry either.*
I nod and grab my things, walk out like I want to walk back in
and say something. But what is there to say?

CIRCLE K BLUES

Trust me, I say, *there's two bucks at least.*
But the old black lady cashier seems happy
to count my pennies. She says, *Ain't no
matter, gotta count 'em nohow.* This takes

a few minutes. Behind her, the cigarettes hum
and the porn rack moans. An Icehouse tall boy
sweats in my palm. She stops at 107, dumps
the rest in the UNICEF jar, gives me this look.

I sigh, *That's cool*, dance out the door
past a girl with tight calves on tall heels
who waves at me from inside as I unlock
my bike. Or is she waving at the Chihuahua

in the Volvo licking the windshield? Sweet Jesus!
P.F. Chang's in the backseat, two bottles of Möet,
and what looks like strawberry cheesecake!

THING IS, I LOVE SPICY FOOD

Tire going flat, I walk into Speedway thumbing back
over my shoulder: *What's up with the air pump?*

Nothing, the cashier says, *it's downright broke.*

Another guy sits behind the counter like he's on
some kind of break. He seems to want my attention,
coughing like he is and holding the Slim-Jim

that's flushed his face and watered his eyes:
If I'd known it was going to be this spicy!

Because I don't know what the hell I'm doing either,
I tell him I generally stay away from spicy food.

Tell you what, he says. Coughs a little more.

REALLY GOOD SALSA

This elderly couple is sitting in a booth
and they haven't said a word except to the waiter.
Haven't touched their chips. Or their salsa.
The wife fidgets with her purse straps
beneath the table. I think she's listening
to the people in the adjacent booth. They're
drinking margaritas. Carrying on. Over there.
The husband studies the sombrero above him
on the wall. Studies it intensely. Like he owns it.
Like it was his until about a month ago
during a polite afternoon barbecue
when his wife's sister's asshole boyfriend
wore it with the humor he intended to give it,
but forgot to take it off when he left,
leaving the old man's bare scalp to blister in the sun.
I want to go over and take the damn sombrero down
and put it on his head. I want him to put it on
his wife's head.
                    Try the salsa. It's good here.
The kids at that table over there, they love it.
It's all over their clothes. Look. You can understand
from when yours were that young. Where are they,
and why haven't they called?
                         Please say something.
This is fantastic Mexican. Remember!
How about that salsa? The mariachi band?
Your new wristwatch? Or, how you've recently
and completely lost your taste for oats? I mean,

every morning for forty years, and now?
What about your wife's hair? Nice, right?
And that broach! Remind her how you saw it
that day on the subway, how badly you wanted to buy it
from the young woman wearing it who told you,
Here, take it, I'm in love.
                                         Listen. Let's trade
places. I'll sit in your booth. I'll eat your salsa.
I'll smile knowingly at the messy children's parents.
Then I'll point the matter out to your wife
who will appreciate the gesture, and laugh.
I'll be you. Fine. I'll wear the damn sombrero. Padre.

I'M THE ASSHOLE

Brooke wants me to stop writing for five minutes
and talk to her, so she picks up a coaster
from the coffee table, one of the heavy kind,
throws it like a Frisbee from across the room
and knocks over my glass of champagne.
This makes me look up from my notebook
because it's pretty impressive, and she's glaring at me,
not mad yet, just confident I shouldn't be surprised
by her accuracy. Her eyebrows are raised
and her mouth is slightly puckered, meaning: she means
business—but not really. That tune from
The Good, the Bad, and the Ugly pops into my head,
so I whistle it and she slouches, deflated,
and I continue writing. She marches
into the bathroom and I don't know why
because she's back in five seconds and, oh, there it is—
the smell of Nivea lotion. I laugh, that's all,
and she says, "You think you're so clever don't you?"
and I say, "Don't you have papers to grade?"
and she stomps to the stairs and says,
"No sex for you tonight." This time she glares mad,
and as she's going up the steps I hear:
"And don't write that!" I say nothing
and I'm reminded of the other day at the mall—
I was walking down that long hallway
to the restrooms. By the phone booth,
there was a big angry guy holding the phone
except he wasn't talking, he was just standing there,

listening, angry looking. Finally he said something
that surprised me and probably whoever
was on the other end. He said, "Guess what, bitch?
Cat's outta the bag! I'm here at the mall buying
your fucking birthday present!" Then he hung up.
He turned and saw I was eavesdropping
and I had an urge to say *You might as well* really *go
have a drink now*—so I did and so
he punched me in the nose. Then he just stood there
like a salt block. Damn, did I want to lick him back!
But I couldn't do it, because I was the asshole.

CATCH AND RELEASE

My cat is an asshole. Impatient. A little bored. Like me
he keeps going for the glass of Maker's
sitting by my laptop. All evening
I've spurned him away with a spray bottle he fears
not at all, so when Arleaux jumps onto the keyboard
adding "ccvdk" to the end of "neighbor's trashcan,"
I raise him by the scruff
thinking nothing of significance
except maybe how I'd like to bite his small ear
so I do that and he makes the face you make
when you're arrested for public intox—
those far-away, Keith Richards eyes,
as though there's something going on
just not where you're at. *Blame it on the whiskey*
he seems to want to say. Which I can understand
because some years ago I was in Cincinnati
for my buddy Chief's wedding,
and Chief had many close friends
so for best man he chose a cousin to keep things simple,
but that guy turned out to be a dick, I think because
he didn't know Chief as well as we did, Chief's buddies,
and he must've felt a little outflanked
though he was warm enough in Windsor
a week before at the bachelor party
with the strippers he enjoyed having
sit on his mustache. But I wasn't even there
at the bride's folks' in Cincy
two nights before the wedding:

someone left a light on
someone oversmoked the brisket
someone sleepwalked and pissed
on the cousin passed out by the toilet
and someone woke up with a shiner.
Tense apologies that morning. So when I
pulled up that afternoon, everyone on the porch,
Faith No More's "Epic" booming from my car,
sign-of-the-horns out the window, in the air,
anxieties shifted: a scapegoat had arrived. I knew
I'd be blamed for the previous night
sure as I'd been blamed for Chief's other indiscretions:
drunk downtown one evening, debating Pete Rose
and Cooperstown, Chief called his fiancée a cunt,
and she warned him to say it again,
so he called her a twat,
and she poured *my* beer on his head. Elsewhere,
having recently discovered his Army peccadilloes
in Stuttgart with Filipina hookers,
she told my girlfriend where she believed
all *my* money went. Better yet
was the time Chief and I dropped acid
and he disappeared
while I was de-alphabetizing my bookshelves
and loudly singing "blue-blue-blue-red-red-red"
over and over really fast like that
with "blue" in baritone and "red" in tenor.
I found Chief in the basement buried under the laundry,

and he was kind of singing the same thing I was,
over and over, same alternating ranges, except
his words were "I am a man's man. I am a man's man."
He told me to go away, so I went
and wrote "BOMB" in black marker on a shoebox
and sat it near him on the floor.
When he saw it, he pissed himself
which pulled him out in more ways than one,
and he said, a little soberly, "Now I'm not afraid to die."
Later we took the shoebox to a drive-thru carryout
and placed it near the entrance
and hid behind some bushes, whispering
"3-2-1" over and over for an hour.
Nothing happened. Hilarious.
But we were caught, red lights blue lights,
and shortly released, red fish blue fish. I took the blame
because I wrote the letters. So after the ceremony
at the VFW, the mother of the bride
pulled me aside, scolded me for wearing white socks
under my tux, and threatened to cut me off
if it came to that. It came to that in fifteen minutes
as I waltzed with a bottle of champagne
while my date watched and giggled.
My date: a girl I truly cared for, who only a month later
wouldn't buy it anymore
and who at one point even punched me
because she thought I said to.
I might have. We were at the Olive Garden,

and I'd guzzled four or five mango martinis.
As I wept like a child, I was likewise turned on—
I threw off my blazer, told her, "You're right: I'm wrong."
She punched me again for my humility.

TRIAL MEMBERSHIP

They ain't got enough weight in this room for me—
is what that guy curling 90s over there
might be thinking. And the woman
walking in who could kick his ass
wears a t-shirt that says *Get off the couch ladies*
which is what we've finally done,
though my shirt says *Pearl Jam*
and Chief's says *Cat's Eye Saloon.*
We wonder where to begin,
what to work on first.
Chief says, "How about our height, or maybe
our eyesight: didn't this place look bigger
online?" I'm feeling we look like idiots
so I sit down on the pec deck
and do a few half-assed reps.
This bald guy by the free weights could be albino.
To the girl he's spotting on bench press, he says,
"Life's like a football game—
you're either playing on the field
or watching from the stands."
At this the girl laughs and her arms go weak:
"Hugh, get the bar, it's not fucking funny!"
But Hugh thinks it's funny: "Tell me I'm right,
Pam, tell me I'm white." Or maybe he says
something else. Because just then Ratt's
"Round and Round" breaks into chorus
over the gym's Bose speakers,
and I'm thinking if it's going to be this place

I'll need to buy an iPod and powerful headphones.
Or powerful earplugs, an opaque pair of sunglasses.
Chief taps my elbow: "Over there, man,
the big dude." Captain America
calf tattoo, ankle weights, a frat shirt:
You may not like us . . . (front), *But*
your girlfriend does (back).

POSE POEM

Before showering, when I'm naked, making muscles in the mirror, I don't simply pose. Usually I'll pretend I'm banging a broad from behind, really hammering it home, one hand gripping her hip and the other on her tramp stamp, stabilizing things, triceps flexed. Either that or I'll act out a sort of take-down, you know, the motion I'd use if I had to defend my mother's life, or something. This involves gripping an invisible neck, wrenching it into a headlock, jabbing the invisible face with typewriter-like snaps of my fist. Whap-whap-whap. I'm five-feet-eleven. And two-thirds. One eighty-five give or take. So when the five-nine one-sixty sonofabitch lunges for my dear mother with a crowbar, it ain't no thing for me to take him down like so. Or, like so. No, like so. That's right. Because I'm in the mirror. The *me* is. Probably six-feet. Probably one-ninety. Making muscles and wrenching headlocks. Hammering home. Keeping things stable. And when I go like this, or maybe like this. . . .

Increasingly I suspect that the poetic sense of the moment described above (me, naked, making muscles in the mirror) is not being conveyed. Maybe the poetic sense simply isn't available to me, either, for one reason or another. Too little imagination. Too much cheap wine. Or, perhaps, making muscles in the mirror while nude is not, could never be, poetic. If my failure to find the poetry in BROCK GUTHRIE NAKED MAKING

MUSCLES IN THE MIRROR is due, in fact, to an *inherent lack* of the poetic therein, then I apologize with total sincerity and vow to remain vigilant. Worthier poetic moments abound.

A GOOD MOMENT

Out there, in the neighbor's driveway,
two gray squirrels snicker on a pile
of dried corn. Not far from that, a dry,
flattened dove. What's left of its wings
flutter in accord with a passing SUV.
In here, Brooke and I are watching
a documentary on voluntary eunuchs.
Who they are, why they do it. Last of his kind,
some old surgeon performs these things
right there in his Brooklyn apartment,
and his neighbors, a young couple
on the brownstone's stoop, have no idea
what he does in 314, but they both admit
the old doc's a pretty good guy.
When told, they're like, *Oh hell no*,
and the boyfriend goes, *I always wanted to ask but . . .*
and Brooke interjects, "I didn't have the balls."
I almost laugh hard. Then think about it:
"OK, that's funny, but I'm not
going to laugh anymore at that kind of joke
because I think you can do better."
At this Brooke laughs even harder than I did,
and I feel an impulse to really put it out there,
so I say, "You know, as soon as you said that,
'I didn't have the balls,' I thought to myself—
*I should tell her I'm not going to
laugh anymore at that kind of joke
because I think she can do better*

—so I told you, hoping to elicit a deeper kind of laughter and, clearly, it worked." Now she thinks I planned the whole thing. Now she thinks I'm the one who, in fact, said, *I didn't have the balls.* She pouts playfully, pounds her fists. I tickle her. It's not a bad moment.

ODE TO STANLEY

Stanley wears a baseball helmet for the hell of it, argues
with his landlord over where to grow his marijuana.
"Not on my property," the landlord says. But the landlord's
nephew mows the grass on Saturdays. "A bucket
in the bed of your pickup is *technically* on my property,"
the landlord calls to say one Sunday. Stanley bikes
up his backroad looking for a spot to transplant the pot,
a clandestine spot with above-average sunlight. Instead

he finds a freshly-dead red fox on the side of the road.
Stanley raises the fox by its thin hind leg, holds it high
like the prize he thinks it is, smiles for three girls driving by
in a convertible—their fresh faces spoil. Stanley's
embarrassed, spits on his shoe, but in a moment of clarity
takes the fox to his landlord's doorstep, leaves a note:
Thought you could think of a better place to put this.

LUKEWARM COFFEE

When the car mechanic tells you an hour,
you never really know. You just give him
your lonely key and sit down
with the others, try to mind your business.
I hate it when there's a TV in the waiting area.
It's always Fox News or some court show
with the judge who thinks
she's funny. But I love it when
there's an old Bunn coffee maker
with fake wood panels and a spot on top
for warming the decaf pot.
It resembles my '88 Wagoneer
if an orange-lipped decanter sat on its roof
and it ran more reliably. I hate it when
there isn't any real half-&-half,
just a canister of powdered cream
which requires extra stirring. But I love it when
real sugar packets are provided
and I'll pour a lot of those into my little Styrofoam cup.
I always take two stirrers.
I hold them like mini chopsticks
when I stir my coffee, pinching the clumps
of powdered cream so they fully dissolve.
It doesn't take long,
in those little Styrofoam cups, for my coffee
to get lukewarm like I like it.
This morning at Firestone it was Fox News,
bummer, but hooray plenty of coffee.

Some guy two chairs over was drinking coffee,
too. He wore a Crimson Tide hat.
He was really watching that TV.
An older black man two chairs farther
was eating chicken pot pie
from a plastic platter tray.
Sarah Palin came on, something about,
oh I don't know, and the black man shook
his head and kept eating, and I tried to see
the Bama guy without his seeing me do so
but I think he saw me.
Boy, was he watching that TV.
I stirred my coffee.
Then I leaned back and looked around him
toward the clock on the wall.
Blew up my cheeks.
Made my eyes real big.
The guy kept watching TV. Only,
like he wanted to say something.
I pinched my powder clumps.
He took off his hat,
slapped his knee, said, *You know what?*
Why don't we give this woman
a goddamn chance! Send her overseas,
let her flirt with these foreign leaders.
She could give 'em all blow jobs!
The black man chuckled
but it was looking more and more

like he couldn't hear too well. Me,
I was thinking back to the beginning
of this little speech. Right after
he said, *You know what?* How I was relieved
I wasn't the only one waiting
for his car. And wouldn't have to
respond with "Roll Tide," or whatever.
But after he said the thing about blow jobs,
I wouldn't really have minded.
Because at least he wasn't praising
Sarah Palin as a person. Not really.

THE LONG RUN

This morning, Nippert comes downstairs
combing his wet hair, puts on his sneakers,
takes a duffel bag from the closet,
spins around, shuffles his feet,
and shimmies out the back door
which swings and creaks against the rusty hinge.
Five, ten seconds tops.
What the hell was that? I ask Adam,
who tells me Nippert's off to shoot
paintball guns with his nephew, Billy,
for little Billy's birthday.
But isn't Billy four? I say,
and he says, *That's right, he's four,
so what's your point?*
and I say, *Nothing,*
and he says, *Teach 'em early is the best way,
safer in the long run.*
Adam goes into the kitchen,
heats up a bowl of venison chili,
comes back and says, *Really,
much safer in the long run.*
His chili smells good. I say, *I think you're right.*
He says, *Pellet guns, 22s—small arms and such.*
I say, *I can't agree more,*
and he says, *What are you saying?* and I say,
Crossbows, throwing stars, hand grenades, tanks.
He says, *Is this because I'm NRA?*
and I ask him if Nippert should grab a pizza

on his way home. He calls me
a terrorist, says, *It's you that's wrong
with this country*, so I say,
*You mean "you're" what's wrong
with this country*, and he says,
*Of course you'd think that,
because it's you that's wrong with this country.*
So I tell him I have a bomb in my shoe.
Liberal, he says. *Just kidding*, I say.
Liberal, he says.

SMALL BAR

When I walk into a small country bar in a small Texas town—
my Stafford shirt collar loosened, neck-tie curled
in my coat pocket—I can tell right away which cowboy
at the bar might like to kick my ass. Up front here,
a twenty-something redhead who ought to be in pictures
tells me to fuck off without exactly saying it.
Her dude leans over the pool table. Fiftyish, he sinks the shot,
straightens, removes his cigarette, then sees me
without exactly looking. The room is antipathetically
smoky. The only person behind the bar
is sitting on a stool with a Martin guitar
and I'll be damned if just as I put my cash on the counter
he doesn't begin "I've Got Rights" by Hank Williams Jr.,
singing in an easy baritone to a bar row of five
and a corner booth of about three.
That the bartender? I ask of a six-and-a-half-foot man
I soon find out but already kind of figured
is the owner of Cotton's Bar and Grill. Cotton tells me
Hank will be over when the song's up, which is fine
because I'm in no hurry. I've got a motel down the road,
and my meeting isn't until two o'clock tomorrow.
I look over the hard liquors as Hank plays that number
and another, order Old Milwaukee instead
which I think is a good choice
because a husky voice somewhere down the bar says
Good choice man
                      but then I hear
Really—good choice

                          only this time more forceful
as if my initial nod was inadequate or
offensive here in this small bar.
This is the cowboy I mentioned earlier.
How to respond?

*Thanks man I truly like this beer it's what I drink
in Ohio when I hunt but it's whiskey when I fish
many trout in Tongue River north of town?*

Or, less tactful:

*Look fucker my folks didn't get along either
and my stepdad, the bastard, looked an awful lot like you.*

But I'm in no mood to chat.

SAINT RANDY
OF THE
SODDEN BAR NAPKIN

ALL THAT WATER

Outdoor bar on a pier at the end of the world, the waitress
seems to be flirting with Nate, but how would he notice?
Late on his mortgage, his doctor told him *gout*, and his dog
got run over. I'm here to buy him a beer. We drink three,
and I suggest time's power to dull, half-knowing
it's the wrong thing to say or maybe the wrong time
to say it, so I fashion a shape with a napkin on the table,
stick a golf ball beneath: it's a crab waddling around.
Four tequila shots, and the wind blows our french fries
off the table. Seven or eight seagulls are nothing
to laugh at. Nate's good with wood, so I ask him to someday
make me a club with my initials on the knob. "I really
wanted those fries," he replies. We walk down the pier.
Congrats are in order for our making good time
into 30-knot winds: "High five, Nate! No? No problem."
Whitecaps compel me to propose we dive, damn right,
head first, down there smack dab between the old pier's
posts—it's all my idea (I'd seen us on shore, windless,
hilarious, two soggy champions) but who holds our stuff?
Instead we smoke on the railing, spit in the sea. Shrimp boats,
discouraged, glide slowly for bay. The awkward brown
pelicans plunge-dive for food, controlled crash-landings—
graceful, actually. I point to the horizon, remind Nate
it's a perfect line. He pisses diagonally into the wind, says,
"Check out my tiny dribble down there in all that water."

SHIVER

In a dark bar that sells breakfast, we're eating it
on a sixty-degree Saturday morning in December.
Kelly says, "Let's drink PBR down at White's Mill!"
and Paul says, "You mean down by the waterfall?"
and Kelly says, "Yeah we'll have a good time,
have a good time." But the Budweiser neon's
red and white light shines down across the bar
and I lean back with my feet up and remember
how she smelled, and Paul tells me I'm wearing
kickball shoes which is a funny thing to say
because he might be right. Kelly tries a joke:
"A man walks into a bar, asks where his friends are,
and the bartender gives him a shot and a beer."
Paul looks so sad now he's watching tennis on TV
and says, "I think last night I was truly happy
at one point," and I say, "I know what you mean,
I remember it like it was yesterday." Kelly suggests
there aren't enough hours in one day; he'll have to
switch to something harder, or go far away
like Uganda or somewhere. I give him my best
Brando: "Don't go, you got your whole life to drink,"
and signal the barmaid, a cheerful thirty-something
whose peach voice alone makes her sufficiently
attractive: "Got a pen?" On the edge of our receipt,
I write a line about the weather, cap the pen
and give it back with a serious "thank you."
She gives a charmed look, and I suddenly feel
momentous, then abashed, and the woman

to my right asks the woman to her right
if her kids have had chicken-pox. She'd like to
expose hers early. I shiver and look at my friends
to see if they heard the remark, but Kelly's scratching
his back with a beer bottle while Paul grins
and gestures grandly: "The catfish was about yea long."

FISHING WITH PAUL

Weaning off a week-long bender, committed
to stretching a half-pint of Jameson over
three full hours, we were perched, parched,
on a log in a clearing among the desiccated
cattails, our bobbers on the pond bobbing
now and then, just enough to keep my gaze
a little crazy and my half-frown fixed. At our feet,
a hand-cranked radio played the golden oldies
amid mundane advertisements like the one
for a retirement village: *Endless Acres.*
"Isn't it strange," I ventured, "how even
the names of insane asylums are peaceful?"
But I couldn't think of any. Maybe I was wrong.
Paul said, "It's called irony," and I didn't disagree.
Then I thought of a word I've always liked
but had heard only lately, though often,
oddly, like a day of rain in the middle
of a drought: *salve.* So I tried to convince Paul
that in language, like life, we unknowingly
revisit certain themes now and again:
"Our ears, our lives, find old sounds
and circumstances, then make them new,
sometimes just by finding them." I was nowhere
and I knew it. Mosquitoes were swarming.
Paul said, "I get it. Like how every time
we come fishing I get poison ivy
and you get these half-baked epiphanies."
Paul was scowling now, shooting fire ants

with a finger-gun: "Kapow, kapow." I thought
I'd try a joke. "Knock-knock," I said. "Who's there?"
I hadn't thought that far ahead.
                              "Camera," I guessed.
"Camera who?"
                         I reeled in my line
like an answer from the deep. "Camera man,"
I guessed again, "camera man sure as hell
wouldn't shoot those ants with a finger-gun."
Paul stopped shooting, affected a Southern drawl
and said, "What we've got here . . . is failure
to communicate." Paul always says that.

WATCH THOSE PMs

Vince tells me he drinks himself to sleep each night
with four or five Tylenol PMs, chases them down
with his seventh or eighth beer.

These figures, he explains, are up from last month
by one or two pills, two or three beers.

All I say is, *Yep*, and he says, *Whoa whoa whoa—
you were thirty, thirty-one, before you slowed down—
I've still got a few years before I really have to worry.*

And I say, *That's fine. Just watch those PMs: you'll grow
so accustomed to that nightly KO—it's a hard routine
to reverse, a very disturbing process.*

And he assures me, *Nah, when it's time to break the spell,
I'll just lay there at night, sleepless with my thoughts.*

Yeah, I tell him, *you sure as hell will.*

ANNA NICOLE HAS COLLAPSED

I was weeping anyway and worrying
down the egg and cheese biscuit
you made before you left but you
forgot the cheese so it was really
just an egg biscuit and the yolk-
yellow Komatsu crane hummed and
dismantled the home across the street
and often wailed for reversal
plus my brain was acting exactly
like that crane and a hard hat
knocked at 2:45 wanting to know
"Can we remove those live oak limbs"
which meant there were chainsaws
broken Mardi Gras beads
and suddenly I see a news crawl:
ANNA NICOLE SMITH HAS DIED
there is no snow in Hollywood Florida
there is no now in Hollywood
and here in New Orleans I feel
a flutter in my chest oh Anna
I'm tired of all this in a way
we loved you show us your tits

SOMETHING TO LOOK AT

On the TV talk show, a dispute
over a fourteen-year-old boy
who made a ten-year-old girl
nervous enough to tell someone.

One woman on the panel
can't get a word in. Another man
of substantial renown thinks
the boy should be put away,
taught a "good, hard lesson."

The crowd applauds but there's
something in his tone: one could say
he isn't sure, that his sentiments
are ceremonial. And the host

won't budge: "They're ten and fourteen—
it was just a simple brush-up
and a complicated complaint."

"Let's be honest," he jokes, "there
wasn't even time for an erection."

Later, on the news, a mother
drowned her five kids. The oldest one
struggled, thought he had a choice.

Chris isn't moved: "All this shit
is tired." With his phone to his thigh
he asks, "Pepperoni?" of Sarah
who looks over at Vince, shakes
her head, and says, "Tired of it."

Vince says, "For you, Sarah,"
pretends to play a tiny violin.

Brooke tells me there's a damp spot
on the rug. I tell her I know:
"There's a seal leak by the skylight
I've been ignoring for months."

I climb to the roof. Poke around.
Smoke. The gutters need cleaning.
I'm throwing leaves everywhere.

Just down the road, something
to look at—the pizza driver braking
to lend a rabbit its ridiculous will.

ROOFER

In my twenty-first year
I was generally fine
while on the roof or
on the way to the roof

but one Monday
the landlord I worked for
told me to paint
the forty-foot eaves

this meant standing
on a narrow rung
near the top of
a collapsible ladder

and reaching left
and right with a brush
while securing
a cup full of paint

no spray gun or safety
harness in that two-bit
operation I'd have to

aim for the bushes
if it came to that

he said if I was scared
it was no big deal
he'd shift me to sewage
or asbestos removal

If you're scared
he said again
I won't make you do it
if you're scared

I'll just find someone
else someone
who ain't scared

I was failing out
of college sleeping
on sofas walking
everywhere I needed to go

this guy owned
half the buildings in town
bought Corvettes
for his sons' girlfriends

pretty sure he had a stake
in the local coke trade too
and who was I

to reason with him okay
so maybe I was a little
scared though
I preferred to believe
that with all his fast
talk and big money

he was compensating
for a tiny something
or other

but I made my living
on top of a roof
I always thought that
sort of thing back then.

APPROPRIATE INTERJECTION

Seven in the morning laying insulation
and wiring electric with a friend and his friend
who make money building houses.
Laying insulation at seven on Saturday
because of a promise made the night before
at the bar where the ambition to learn
something about house circuitry
appeared like a blown fuse. This pink shit
makes you itchy. Not so with my friend here—
he's worked with this stuff so long
he sleeps on it, wakes up,
throws a piece in the toaster, eats it slowly
with cream cheese and coffee. Shouldn't we
be wearing respirators or something?
How the hell should I know?
But this is good. This kind of work
is good for me—re-callous these grandma hands
I've grown. Like back in those summers
when I tar-sealed blacktop
on ninety-five degree early mornings. "And then
in the afternoons," I tell them. On break
we smoke a joint in front of the site, drink
water, sit there in silence. Silent like that
until I start to count breaths. And wonder
what happened to last night's beer brotherhood.
But then I recognize the similarity
between our collective awareness
and the object of our unfocused gazes:

Margaret's Creek running muddy and a little high
along the other side of the road.
I could try to articulate this thought—
it might break the silence. Then again it might
make more. And I want to work with these guys
on future jobs, so instead I tell them how
I once caught a five-pound largemouth
a quarter-mile up this creek
that jerked so hard in my grip
she stuck two of the treble hook barbs
from the top-water Rapala I caught her with
into my thumb, how I tried for an hour
to loosen them from the nerve, feeling it
in my front teeth, fish in the water, gone,
how I had to push the points
clear through the side of my thumb
and clip the barbs with rusty wire cutters.
"Sure," I add, "there's good fishing in this creek
if you know the good holes."
Then my friend's friend holds out his left thumb,
a nubby little thing, tells us about an accident
he had with a circular saw.

HE QUITS HIS BLUE-COLLAR JOB

He walks right into the office, uses the word *menial*,
then walks out whistling, feeling nervously loose
the way a beautiful woman can make men
speak or be speechless, make us pause
at the gas station, say hello or nothing at all.
Then it starts raining, and he thinks of Raskolnikov
at the bar, early in the book, confounded,
but how after one drink, clarity came
to pluck him back up so he could ripen
for another fall. Feeling relatively benign, however,
he walks into the Smiling Skull Saloon, paper under his arm,
nods reluctantly to a guy in the corner he knows
who's become so misanthropic he ends conversations
with head-butts. Then he orders a beer
and says *menial* glibly to the barmaid who smiles
in a way that makes him think she's heard something
truly profound. And when the drunk across the bar
shouts *amen* he thinks *beggary* and senses
he shouldn't write his wealthy bereaving aunt,
so he opens . . . closes the classifieds, drinks his beer,
and drives home, suddenly alarmed and slightly
panicked over what might be in his mailbox,
whose voice on his answering machine.

CANDY DISH

I never go to funerals before a bourbon shot or two.
Funeral homes: they're clean, they're crisp.
I'm anxious and a little sour.
I think I need a breath mint.
Dear candy dish, in you I always find
what passes for a breath mint.
You're the first thing I see
when I step lightly into the calling hours. Immediately
I want to dump all your contents in my pocket
and run away. Or put you on my head. Or hold you
to my chin and turn to the nearest mourner
and say, "Check out my new beard!"
But that would be ridiculous so I simply admire you
as you are, so full
under the green parlor lamp
next to where we sign our names. I sign
and take a handful. There's no one here
I know except you. You
and a colleague whose mother is the honored dead,
whose father died a year ago, who's
twenty-seven, kind, deleteriously uncynical,
and receiving yet another long,
ephemeral line of well-wishers—
rather casually-dressed callers including
six to eight vibrant women
wearing an assortment of sweet colors
like saccharine black,
but the one who seems especially alive

is wearing blue, backless, flowered. She's blonde
and apparently, turning now—baby fattened.
Above her, six panes of stained glass. Each
bears a message and a biblical image.
Here's a goat and words. A wine goblet
and words. Here's one
with the sun beaming through showing
Christ with unquiet eyes
and around him in a curiously strong font
more words: *Why are you fearful, O ye of little faith?*
Here's the mother. Bigger lady, she likely enjoyed
cinnamon and cherry and licorice
and pork and cake. No doubt
we could have found you, candy dish, half-full
in various rooms of her home
and you empty in some of her drawers,
but unlike you, I've never met this woman
lying here whose face is kind—
she looks like she's sleeping.
I've only known her son
for about a month through work,
but I think we've shared enough
in the way of sports braggadocio and car troubles
to justify my appearance here at the casket.
We even played golf, once, a few weeks back.
His swing needed work, and I told him so.
He'd probably given it about as much thought
as he's had removing you

from his mother's home. After golf, we had beers
in a local bar. Several drinkers asked him
about his mother's health, but no one really listened
as he tried to explain, so I can't help but worry
he'll mistake my intentions here
since he knows enough about me to plausibly assume
I stopped by for "material."
(Oh Jesus, since when was this about me?)
But then I meet him in line,
put out my hand, assume a solemn, thin-lipped face
like William Hurt in *The Big Chill*,
and slip him Brach's butterscotch. He smiles!
You candy dish! Place like this,
I don't see how you can be so full.

LOVING CUP

The shadow of Jesus Christ at night
spread wide across the northwest side
of St. Louis Cathedral in the Quarter
is a thing to behold, so
I let my folks stroll ahead to behold it
while I stop at a gallery window on Royal
to regard the greatest photographed
ass I've ever seen: black and white,
woman stretched belly down on a bed
lying lengthwise away from us
with the covers pulled to the bottom
of her crack—in the background we see
her teased black hair on the pillow
her arms are tucked under, but her back
curves down and out of view, blooming
her ass like an apple for the foreground. Oh,
I've always been one for posteriors, but
to sit at her side in that unexposed margin,
to witness the inverted arc, the ungodly
chalice, with a go-cup from Molly's
full of Maker's and ice . . .

RELIGION

After another four-day bender—
your mood's stable, stomach's settled,

appetite's strong, and you can sit still
long enough to watch *Jimmy Swaggart*.

Plus you have the will to write a line about it!
Maybe you think you're qualified now

to assume the Chair of the Committee
for Innocuous Inebriation. You would be

mistaken because (knowing Sunday
is your day to wean, that by six or seven

everything right with you goes wrong) the one
who walked your dog before bringing you

biscuits in bed with an Alka-Seltzer
will drive at five across the Mississippi

to West Baton Rouge, nearest parish
selling spirits on a holy day, to fetch

a pint of Jim Beam which makes her
not only the C.I.I. chair but also

a loyal parishioner at the Church
of Placid Midnights where you're forever

St. Randy of the Sodden Bar Napkin.
Try hard to worship her, too. Son.

THE WAGON

When you've forgotten enough
as to believe in here and now

the day ahead sits apple-mouthed
the core of a week in a sweet slow year

and your grass-stained sneakers remind you
the backyard needs mowing

but the mower's missing a wheel
and the local hardware store
ain't hardly that

and Home Depot's twenty miles out
plus your truck's on empty and besides
it looks like rain sweet rain

once again it comes to this
wedged like an hour in the night of your freezer
is a Smirnoff pint you'll ignore or you won't

ERRANDS

ONCE I GET UP THIS HILL

Prolific, the snow, this winter in Boston, perpendicular
snow-year, like maybe a record, so I called Paul there
to hear what he thought of the Vancouver Olympics,
but really I'd been sleepless for three or four days
on a feasible detox bending inward by the hour
and Paul had a method, some concoction or other
of sunlight and something Woody Guthrie and whatnot
and I needed reminding, but Paul was on his bike,
two lobsters in his backpack, at the base of a hill
in Brighton, bracing for the climb. The hill was
Bigelow. He said, "I truly love my ruby's smile."
I could hear in his voice he was squinting at the hill
like he was staring at the sun, and this was something
he did daily with a childlike sort of dread, since,
at the top—his basement apartment, an old sheepdog
in diapers, last of the Percocet for his severed
thumb-muscle, latest arduous email from his father
with Parkinson's, and his auburn-haired Erin who
cooks a mean lobster, so that bit about the smile? Not so
random, rather moving. I pictured Madison Avenue—
a steep street and hillside we'd snowboard those winters
of our stoned adolescence. Half-hour up, half-minute
down. There was no way around it, this Bigelow hill.
"What say I call you when I get up this hill?" I pictured
millions of people, at that very moment, needing to reach
the top of some hill. "I'll feel much better once I get up
this hill." How could I argue? "Call me then," I said.

CLEVER FISH

That winter in Baltimore our kitchen
was drafty. Creditors kept our phone
alive like crickets. Beneath our sink,
maybe a bong. Sometimes at night
I'd see myself in the window, consider
cutting my hair, going back
to school. But I'd have been happy
had you simply valued seafood.
Something about the texture and taste
you found "obnoxious." Oh, you'd eat
crab cakes (with cocktail sauce and wine)
and once, I grilled salmon and you tried it,
made no face. Snow to the windows
one night in December. A gift
arrived at our door! Your cousin
Tony in a faux-fur Cossack
with a twelve of Sam Adams
and a bushel of blue crab, an old Chesapeake
recipe, and this was getting serious
so I told you that you and the sea
were harmonious, showing my favorite picture:
a photo I kept in a case on my key ring
of you in a sundress, kneeling in the surf
on a Connecticut shore. You flipped it over,
gave me a look: another one I took
of a King Mackerel I'd caught, cigar
in its mouth, little sunglasses on.

POETRY

The other day at a smart coffee shop, I was revising my
          grocery list
when I overheard a couple arguing in borderline whispers

about another couple, how *that* guy writes poems for *his*
          girlfriend,
like the one he showed them that was "coarse but clever."

"You could write a song," I heard her suggest. So he said,
          "Okay. Fine.
Good idea. I'll go to the mall and buy strings for my guitar."

AIRPLANE ASSHOLE

I want a Martin Backpacker
acoustic guitar—travel size,
so I could play it

on a commercial flight.
When asking for the cabin's
permission, because

it's the mindful thing to do,
I figure some old Republican
would make a big scene.

But then I could easily
turn it around
on that guy. I'd be like:

*Yeah right, man, like I'm
really going to sit here
and play a guitar on an*

*airplane. Asshole. Shut up
and drink your orange juice.*

Now he has to live with that.
Now he has to live that down
for the rest of the flight

because now more than a few
really do want to hear me
play that little guitar,

and they're mad as hell
and so are the folks who
don't care this way or that,

who are simply siding
with the Yeas because
they're younger, wear

slightly ironic shoes,
and include a brown-eyed
girl in her mid-to-late twenties

who's been smiling a lot,
reading Barthes' *Mythologies*,
sipping Miller Genuine Draft.

She seems to know
something else
because of all that.

ANTIZIGZAG

I stood near an ATM on Iberville
and the bum who seemed asleep
in the neighboring stoop said
I wouldn't do that if I were you

so I nodded and gave him a dollar
and sunk into my last three drinks
deep enough to think I might try it sometime

sit in a stoop for as long as I can
move to another and sit there and move
find ways to pass the days
lacking cash and clean teeth but

to speak elliptically to people with wallets
and imagine my words sailing safely on through

but then I recalled I'd doubled thirty at Harrah's
and reconsidered my immediate needs
since the ripe August wind was so brackish and clammy
and boiled crawfish breezed out of Felix's Oyster Bar

plus the girl with me wore
lipstick and beads and black leather knee-highs
we both made a beeline in.

ERRANDS

Brooke sent me into Walgreens to buy an EPT
and I was concerned about that
but a guy in his car next spot over
was looking at a vagina
enveloping a midget's fist
right there with his window down
and the magazine spread across the steering wheel
of his late model Lexus. I stood there
staring, uneasy, almost hoping
he'd notice me
in which case I might have winked and said,
"Man, that's a good one,"
or something encouraging like that
because something should be said,
but what is that something? But this guy
was so absorbed by the porn
he didn't give a shit who saw,
so I walked into Walgreens feeling conflicted—
good thing he didn't see me, right?
Good thing I didn't say what I might have—
but when I came out of Walgreens with the EPT,
he was still looking intensely
at two-dimensional sex
and there was no one in the store meaning
no one to wait for
and both his hands held the magazine
so I figured it was simply some kind of fetish,
browsing pornography in public—

a way to exhibit what I should neither
condemn nor understand.
And that was that.
I lit a cigarette.
We ran other errands.
Half-hour later we drove past Walgreens
and stopped at a red light just down the road
near Southdowns Preschool playground
where we saw the Lexus and the same guy inside
waving with his free hand
at two boys no older than five
whose lunch boxes lay in the dirt.
I smacked the Walgreens bag from Brooke's lap
so I could grab her leg. She grabbed her cell phone,
flipped it open, and asked me "Should I?"
I said, "I don't know,"
and she asked me again
and I promised, "I think so."

SHH... WE'RE TRYING TO FOCUS IN HERE

My roommate said he'd buy cigarettes for a week
if I went to his postcolonial literature class
and took notes, so I did, and the professor
and the handful of students paying attention
were really delving into some character
named "Slavesister" in a novel whose subject
was the Indian partition of 1947
and the massacres that followed, but their voices
were stifled by the sounds from the hallway,
a different sort of debate, I gathered,
by the volume and range of inflection.
They were the black women custodians,
and their generous chitchat was clearly a way
to pass the menial day, but it was distracting, really,
so much so that an older white woman
I'd already pegged for earnestness in all matters
went out and said something, but when she came back
the chitchat continued, got a little louder,
strengthened most likely by what these custodians
might have been thinking: "Fuck that bitch."
This idea disturbed me, and I was trying
to work out why when it suddenly didn't seem
to matter: the professor was from Mumbai,
wore a red and gold sari, and she went to the hall
to try the same thing only this time it worked.
One custodian said "Sorry." What a relief!
What a fitting resolution and finally I could focus
on what was really going on: a delving into Slavesister
and the Indian partition of 1947.

JULY FOURTH

Chuck's ten-acre spread with a one-story
farmhouse, one-acre pond, grass half court
with a hoop on the barn, and a crescent
moon cutout in the door of the outhouse
so when you shit there's still a little light.
Turkey shoot was all Paulette, third year in a row,
Emily handed Tony his ass in one-on-one,
and we all agreed Chuck's marrow burgers
could use more Lea & Perrins. Drowsing
by the fire pit, all but me and Grippa,
we're backing down the driveway on a run
for beer and foil. Grippa's rolling a number
and can't be sure what I mean when I say,
"Well, fuck me, Kennedy's dead."
The family cat, the strong male—
ten-year survivor of this 60-limit stretch of 646,
his hunting grounds the high grass beyond
this two-lane—sprawled dead on solid yellows.
Just an hour earlier I was up at the pond
slaying bluegill, crappie, thinking it weird
he wasn't weaving my ankles, angling for handouts.
Grippa's by the truck. I'm at the cat.
A shock of fur rips away clean before I think
to grab a leg. His whole side is split, a wound
rimmed with cinders. I lay him under a bush
and go tell Chuck who isn't too impressed,
he's seen it before, fetches a shovel as Grandma,
89, seasoned by circumstance, exempt
from high drama, looks at the stain on the asphalt,

the field of high grass beyond, and the sun
barely visible above the tree line. She asks me
where little Izaak is or if he knows yet.
I don't think so. Me and Grippa
take backroads to get those beers and foil.
In the parking lot of Bob's Pic-Pac,
Grippa's ashing out, I'm checking my eyes
in the rearview, a hummingbird flies
into the truck's open window, hovers there
above the dash for a second, then blurs away
leaving us stoned and searching for words.
"That was the second biggest bumblebee
I've seen today," says Grippa, and we pause
to consider his deadpan. "Or maybe
it's the dark," I say. "Birds are crazy
near dusk, alarmed because they forget
to expect night. Same with old folks, only
different, how some grow bitter near the end,
facing the unknown, the darkness
but with a shade of acceptance."
Grippa's a skeptic: "Why are birds afraid
of the dark?" and I almost say
"because of surreptitious felines"
but I know this isn't accurate, and I'd feel guilty
if he laughs too hard, so I say nothing,
and on the way home, we buy fireworks
from the only roadside vendor in town,
a man content to sit there, spit, wait

for the darkness that comes once a year
so he can see his livelihood light up the sky.

ANIMALS

"One is what one looks at—well, at least partially."
—Joseph Brodsky

All morning in my hammock burning
a tight one, poised with pencil and notebook
and seven-week beard, I look to the pines
outside my cabin seeking inspiration
from the birds and the squirrels
whose singing and foraging, whose
exclamations, no, arguments, reflect
my inner my inner my inner . . .
and every so often my cousin Ricky returns
from hunting rabbits on my four-wheeler
to tell me he's thought of a new way
to beat off: *Anywhere around here to buy
watermelons?* Even his camo flannel
can't conceal that Superdome belly
and I hate to think how long
since anyone's seen his diminutive dangle,
so I tell him in all seriousness, my sympathy
sincere, *You might be on to something,*
but after he tokes and rides away,
I get inspired, realize I should've said,
*Go drive around these country roads, man,
look for signs!* and even Ricky would've
nodded with a look of feigned profundity
like he's posing for an author photo,
but I let that moment go
in order to capture the moment of *me*

alone with the foraging squirrels
and their question-mark tails, the birds
whose names I never learned
to remember. Yet why not simply see it?
Why not say what happens? Forgive me just now
if I feel a little sheepish (*question-mark tails?*),
if I feel a little guilt-sick for my under-
used brain, the old poetic pathways
so infrequently travelled that, too easily,
on warm days like these
when I find myself finally ass-in-hammock
with a will to invent, the mind's ice melt
evades the deadfall of word-alchemy
to seek instead the well-carved rivulets of
roll-another-joint-and-drink-another-beer
that feed the Netflix stream
into the Ocean of Ohfuckit
till I'm all, like, totally
washed up on the Jersey Shore. Or surfing
my iPad on a YouTube. No surprise, then,
when Ricky rides up all boots and burrs
with his iPhone out and a video to share:
*Check it out, brah, she puts Sriracha on it
before it goes in.* If I tell him I'd rather be
roadkill, a heap of broken armor
for a crowd of sarcastic crows, than ogle

fetish porn on another man's cell phone
does he still announce with equal aplomb
that he's *just come from seeing armadillos
banging in the woods like a couple
of rabbits*? and do I ask him to clarify
what he means by *come*? or do I
take a quick peek, close the matter off
with a simple observation that proves
I almost care? *Look, man, I've slept
with fake blondes, and as your video confirms,
they often don't know how to do it.* And yet
I feel a minor buzz in my pants.
But it's a text from my wife: *Don't. Be. Mad.*
Well . . . she's at lunch now
with old MFA friends, a teetotaler couple
from somewhere up north. Of course,
I should be there, but my wife let it slip that
she's writing a series of moon pantoums
and *he*, I don't know, probably writes
about squirrels. Me: *Why what is it?*
Wife: *They need to sleep over.*
Wife: *I couldn't say no.*
Wife: *It'll be fine—he wants to swap poems.*
How do I express, 160 characters or less,
how terrified this makes me? *Then I'll be
out there in the trees with blanket&bottle
&block of headcheese. Send the dogs
in the morning to let me know they're gone.*

The patio door hinge whines again.
If it's Ricky with a porcupine,
I'll cry right now. His hands are empty,
but what about his mind: *I was staring
at this log and I had a weird thought—
the longer you look at something, the more
it looks like you.* Which must be why
this poem is making me nervous.

BRUSH CLEARING

The property had really gone to shit
over the past ten years before we moved in—
a seasonal deer camp for guns and their grown men,
psychedelic weekend retreat for frat boys—
and nothing begun on my end needed
ending, not a single line in weeks,
so I got up early, ate a hard-boiled egg,
drank a little Gatorade, and jumped out my cabin
into the thick Tuscaloosa summer
wearing a green bandana and Caterpillar boots,
shed-bound with a piece of stationery tucked
in the back pocket of my Levi's.
For I had brush to clear.
Here was a list from my wife: nuisance trees
like thorn and privet, aggressive vines
like creeper and kudzu and poison ivy—
cutting all that back is one way
to sweat out yesterday's nightcap
but mainly a means to curb ticks and fleas
and mosquitoes and rashes, well no,
mainly a way to reveal original landscaping—
another list from my wife, what not to cut back:
lily-turf and mondo grass, boxwood and holly,
Carolina rose, crape myrtle, juniper.
I went back inside to Google some terms.
When I emerged once more with something like
a vision, three mockingbirds abandoned
the vine-choked blueberry bush

and perched overhead on a wire to watch me—
I was that consequential
with a two-month beard and an iPod head nod.
Suddenly I felt *okay*.
You could almost say I was *rocking out*.
But that feeling only lasted
till I was aware of it, a lonely line
jotted down in a Moleskine, implied
but undeveloped, irrelevant
by the time I got to the shed
filled with the abandoned tools of former tenants
and, generally, in its clutter, not unlike
my state of mind: a little of this, a little of that,
all of it rusty, foreign, familiar.
On a tall shelf, inside a Walmart bag,
a heavy box portrayed on its sides
a young couple in swimsuits
with a beach ball and two kids, all of them
wet and cool and happy
in an inflatable 500-gallon pool.
I wiped my face and reordered my priorities.
Half hour later I was kneeling on the deck
with my new rusty hammer, pounding popped nails
to smooth the boards for the skin-thin vinyl floor.
The sun was exactly above me—*would be*
above that spot for three hours
each cloudless day for the rest of the summer.
I figured this out.

And that feeling I had earlier returned
because I was thinking now about *tomorrow*—
which was not now and not immediate and therefore
not as much me,
and I knew I'd be okay, tomorrow,
wet and cool and happy
after hours of clearing brush and soon
all would be revealed.
The blueberries would be dark and dusty,
and with fewer fleas and mosquitoes, my dogs
would scratch and bite themselves less.
I would scratch and bite myself less.
And whether I ever
wrote another line or not, this
would be key going forward:
Each day I'll figure something out
to give my loved ones a reason
to believe in me tomorrow.

HALF HOUR

Nippy, vodka drunk, and uninspired, you decide
to switch to beer. You leave your serious bedroom,
see three friends leaving the bathroom,
hear one say, *I was doing it on the way home
in Lancaster traffic.* You go outside to your porch.
Snow falls on your shoulders, your head,
on the rows of stacked silver cans, and on the possum
that tries to burrow into your uncovered trash barrel.
Standing under the bare light bulb,
you're holding it by the scruff, thinking
nothing of significance, except maybe
how it ain't no thing for you to pick up a wild possum
coolly. And hold it there. Your cat walks over curious,
so you pick him up, too, and show him
to the nipply possum. Cat meet Possum.
Nothing happens. They must know each other.
Your cat wants to go inside where it's warmer,
so you put him down, and he runs in
through his cat door. Meanwhile the possum
hangs motionless, is laboring intensely, you imagine,
to hang motionless in your grip like a big boot.
When you blow in her ear she hisses like Dracula,
so you drop her and she burrows
and two of your friends, watching from inside,
decide they've seen enough, go back to the fireplace
where everyone else is. Good for them.
You're in this for something. You can see
the scaly, prehensile tail. When you

brush the marbled gray fur white with your hand,
it stays white like that until you brush it back gray.
Now the possum burrows deeper, nearly out of sight,
so you leave it alone and piss your initials
in the snow off the porch, wishing possum well
and murmuring, softly, *way home, way home,*
way home in Lancaster traffic. Then you sneak
into the guest room upstairs, lock the door,
and fall asleep on the floor reading Chekhov
after thinking how impossible it would be
to convince anyone how important
the past half hour had been.

ACKNOWLEDGMENTS

I am grateful to the editors who first published the following poems in this collection, some in earlier versions:

Cimarron Review: "Errands" (as "The Cherub")

Cold Mountain Review: "Shiver"

DIG: "Thing Is, I Love Spicy Food" and "Poetry"

Iron Horse Literary Review: "Clever Fish" and "Half Hour"

Litrag #14: "He Quits His Blue-Collar Job" and "July Fourth" (as "Birds and Humans")

Los Angeles Review: "Roofer"

New Ohio Review: "Animals" and "Appropriate Interjection"

The Southern Review: "Some Days," "I'm the Asshole," and "Something to Look At"

"Animals" and "Pose Poem" appeared in *FUCK POEMS: An Exceptional Anthology*, from Lavender Ink Press, Vincent A. Cellucci, Editor.

"Clever Fish" was reprinted in the anthology, *Tuscaloosa Writes This*, from Slash Pine Press, Brian Oliu and Patti White, Editors.

GRATITUDE

For their encouragement, guidance, and close reading, thank you to Mark Halliday, Laura Mullen, Megan Volpert, Brooke Champagne, Jill Allyn Rosser, Vincent Cellucci, Christopher Shipman, Paul McNamara, Andrei Codrescu, Bret Lott, and my editors at SRP, Bryan Borland and Seth Pennington. And for their love and support along the way, thank you to Randy and Sandy Guthrie, Diana and Tom Glaizer, Jennifer Wessell, and Paul Merkel.

THE POET

Brock Guthrie was born and raised in Athens, Ohio. He graduated from Ohio University and the M.F.A. program at Louisiana State University. He teaches writing and literature at the University of Alabama in Tuscaloosa.

WWW . **BROCKGUTHRIE** . ORG

Author Photograph: Brooke Champagne

THE PRESS

Founded in 2010, Sibling Rivalry Press is an independent publishing house based in Alexander, Arkansas. Our mission is to publish work that disturbs and enraptures.

www.SIBLINGRIVALRYPRESS.com

www.ingramcontent.com/pod-product-compliance
Lightning Source LLC
LaVergne TN
LVHW062058090426
835512LV00034B/603